Parent Teacher Communication Log

Year at a glance

August	September	October

November	December	January

February	March	April

May	June	July

Student Name	
Parents Name	
Address	
Phone Number	Home: Work:
Email	

Date	
Person Contacted	
Method Of Contact	
Reason	
Notes	

Date	
Person Contacted	
Method Of Contact	
Reason	
Notes	

Date	
Person Contacted	
Method Of Contact	
Reason	
Notes	

Date	
Person Contacted	
Method Of Contact	
Reason	
Notes	

Date	
Person Contacted	
Method Of Contact	
Reason	
Notes	

Student Name	
Parents Name	
Address	
Phone Number	Home: Work:
Email	

Date	
Person Contacted	
Method Of Contact	
Reason	
Notes	

Date	
Person Contacted	
Method Of Contact	
Reason	
Notes	

Date	
Person Contacted	
Method Of Contact	
Reason	
Notes	

Date	
Person Contacted	
Method Of Contact	
Reason	
Notes	

Date	
Person Contacted	
Method Of Contact	
Reason	
Notes	

Student Name	
Parents Name	
Address	
Phone Number	Home: Work:
Email	

Date	
Person Contacted	
Method Of Contact	
Reason	
Notes	

Date	
Person Contacted	
Method Of Contact	
Reason	
Notes	

Date	
Person Contacted	
Method Of Contact	
Reason	

Notes

Date	
Person Contacted	
Method Of Contact	
Reason	

Notes

Date	
Person Contacted	
Method Of Contact	
Reason	

Notes

Student Name	
Parents Name	
Address	
Phone Number	Home: Work:
Email	

Date	
Person Contacted	
Method Of Contact	
Reason	
Notes	

Date	
Person Contacted	
Method Of Contact	
Reason	
Notes	

Date	
Person Contacted	
Method Of Contact	
Reason	
Notes	

Date	
Person Contacted	
Method Of Contact	
Reason	
Notes	

Date	
Person Contacted	
Method Of Contact	
Reason	
Notes	

Student Name	
Parents Name	
Address	
Phone Number	Home: Work:
Email	

Date	
Person Contacted	
Method Of Contact	
Reason	
Notes	

Date	
Person Contacted	
Method Of Contact	
Reason	
Notes	

Date	
Person Contacted	
Method Of Contact	
Reason	
Notes	

Date	
Person Contacted	
Method Of Contact	
Reason	
Notes	

Date	
Person Contacted	
Method Of Contact	
Reason	
Notes	

Student Name	
Parents Name	
Address	
Phone Number	Home: Work:
Email	

Date	
Person Contacted	
Method Of Contact	
Reason	
Notes	

Date	
Person Contacted	
Method Of Contact	
Reason	
Notes	

Date	
Person Contacted	
Method Of Contact	
Reason	
Notes	

Date	
Person Contacted	
Method Of Contact	
Reason	
Notes	

Date	
Person Contacted	
Method Of Contact	
Reason	
Notes	

Student Name	
Parents Name	
Address	
Phone Number	Home: Work:
Email	

Date	
Person Contacted	
Method Of Contact	
Reason	
Notes	

Date	
Person Contacted	
Method Of Contact	
Reason	
Notes	

Date	
Person Contacted	
Method Of Contact	
Reason	
Notes	

Date	
Person Contacted	
Method Of Contact	
Reason	
Notes	

Date	
Person Contacted	
Method Of Contact	
Reason	
Notes	

Student Name	
Parents Name	
Address	
Phone Number	Home: Work:
Email	

Date	
Person Contacted	
Method Of Contact	
Reason	
Notes	

Date	
Person Contacted	
Method Of Contact	
Reason	
Notes	

Date	
Person Contacted	
Method Of Contact	
Reason	
Notes	

Date	
Person Contacted	
Method Of Contact	
Reason	
Notes	

Date	
Person Contacted	
Method Of Contact	
Reason	
Notes	

Student Name	
Parents Name	
Address	
Phone Number	Home: Work:
Email	

Date	
Person Contacted	
Method Of Contact	
Reason	
Notes	

Date	
Person Contacted	
Method Of Contact	
Reason	
Notes	

Date	
Person Contacted	
Method Of Contact	
Reason	

Notes

Date	
Person Contacted	
Method Of Contact	
Reason	

Notes

Date	
Person Contacted	
Method Of Contact	
Reason	

Notes

Student Name		
Parents Name		
Address		
Phone Number	Home:	Work:
Email		

Date	
Person Contacted	
Method Of Contact	
Reason	

Notes

Date	
Person Contacted	
Method Of Contact	
Reason	

Notes

Date	
Person Contacted	
Method Of Contact	
Reason	
Notes	

Date	
Person Contacted	
Method Of Contact	
Reason	
Notes	

Date	
Person Contacted	
Method Of Contact	
Reason	
Notes	

Student Name	
Parents Name	
Address	
Phone Number	Home: Work:
Email	

Date	
Person Contacted	
Method Of Contact	
Reason	
Notes	

Date	
Person Contacted	
Method Of Contact	
Reason	
Notes	

Date	
Person Contacted	
Method Of Contact	
Reason	
Notes	

Date	
Person Contacted	
Method Of Contact	
Reason	
Notes	

Date	
Person Contacted	
Method Of Contact	
Reason	
Notes	

Student Name	
Parents Name	
Address	
Phone Number	Home: Work:
Email	

Date	
Person Contacted	
Method Of Contact	
Reason	
Notes	

Date	
Person Contacted	
Method Of Contact	
Reason	
Notes	

Date	
Person Contacted	
Method Of Contact	
Reason	
Notes	

Date	
Person Contacted	
Method Of Contact	
Reason	
Notes	

Date	
Person Contacted	
Method Of Contact	
Reason	
Notes	

Student Name	
Parents Name	
Address	
Phone Number	Home: Work:
Email	

Date	
Person Contacted	
Method Of Contact	
Reason	
Notes	

Date	
Person Contacted	
Method Of Contact	
Reason	
Notes	

Date	
Person Contacted	
Method Of Contact	
Reason	
Notes	

Date	
Person Contacted	
Method Of Contact	
Reason	
Notes	

Date	
Person Contacted	
Method Of Contact	
Reason	
Notes	

Student Name	
Parents Name	
Address	
Phone Number	Home: Work:
Email	

Date	
Person Contacted	
Method Of Contact	
Reason	
Notes	

Date	
Person Contacted	
Method Of Contact	
Reason	
Notes	

Date	
Person Contacted	
Method Of Contact	
Reason	

Notes

Date	
Person Contacted	
Method Of Contact	
Reason	

Notes

Date	
Person Contacted	
Method Of Contact	
Reason	

Notes

Student Name	
Parents Name	
Address	
Phone Number	Home: Work:
Email	

Date	
Person Contacted	
Method Of Contact	
Reason	
Notes	

Date	
Person Contacted	
Method Of Contact	
Reason	
Notes	

Date	
Person Contacted	
Method Of Contact	
Reason	
Notes	

Date	
Person Contacted	
Method Of Contact	
Reason	
Notes	

Date	
Person Contacted	
Method Of Contact	
Reason	
Notes	

Student Name	
Parents Name	
Address	
Phone Number	Home: Work:
Email	

Date	
Person Contacted	
Method Of Contact	
Reason	
Notes	

Date	
Person Contacted	
Method Of Contact	
Reason	
Notes	

Date	
Person Contacted	
Method Of Contact	
Reason	
Notes	

Date	
Person Contacted	
Method Of Contact	
Reason	
Notes	

Date	
Person Contacted	
Method Of Contact	
Reason	
Notes	

Student Name	
Parents Name	
Address	
Phone Number	Home: Work:
Email	

Date	
Person Contacted	
Method Of Contact	
Reason	
Notes	

Date	
Person Contacted	
Method Of Contact	
Reason	
Notes	

Date	
Person Contacted	
Method Of Contact	
Reason	
Notes	

Date	
Person Contacted	
Method Of Contact	
Reason	
Notes	

Date	
Person Contacted	
Method Of Contact	
Reason	
Notes	

Student Name	
Parents Name	
Address	
Phone Number	Home: Work:
Email	

Date	
Person Contacted	
Method Of Contact	
Reason	
Notes	

Date	
Person Contacted	
Method Of Contact	
Reason	
Notes	

Date	
Person Contacted	
Method Of Contact	
Reason	

Notes

Date	
Person Contacted	
Method Of Contact	
Reason	

Notes

Date	
Person Contacted	
Method Of Contact	
Reason	

Notes

Student Name	
Parents Name	
Address	
Phone Number	Home: Work:
Email	

Date	
Person Contacted	
Method Of Contact	
Reason	
Notes	

Date	
Person Contacted	
Method Of Contact	
Reason	
Notes	

Date	
Person Contacted	
Method Of Contact	
Reason	
Notes	

Date	
Person Contacted	
Method Of Contact	
Reason	
Notes	

Date	
Person Contacted	
Method Of Contact	
Reason	
Notes	

Student Name	
Parents Name	
Address	
Phone Number	Home: Work:
Email	

Date	
Person Contacted	
Method Of Contact	
Reason	
Notes	

Date	
Person Contacted	
Method Of Contact	
Reason	
Notes	

Date	
Person Contacted	
Method Of Contact	
Reason	
Notes	

Date	
Person Contacted	
Method Of Contact	
Reason	
Notes	

Date	
Person Contacted	
Method Of Contact	
Reason	
Notes	

Student Name	
Parents Name	
Address	
Phone Number	Home: Work:
Email	

Date	
Person Contacted	
Method Of Contact	
Reason	

Notes

Date	
Person Contacted	
Method Of Contact	
Reason	

Notes

Date	
Person Contacted	
Method Of Contact	
Reason	

Notes

Date	
Person Contacted	
Method Of Contact	
Reason	

Notes

Date	
Person Contacted	
Method Of Contact	
Reason	

Notes

Student Name	
Parents Name	
Address	
Phone Number	Home: Work:
Email	

Date	
Person Contacted	
Method Of Contact	
Reason	
Notes	

Date	
Person Contacted	
Method Of Contact	
Reason	
Notes	

Date	
Person Contacted	
Method Of Contact	
Reason	

Notes

Date	
Person Contacted	
Method Of Contact	
Reason	

Notes

Date	
Person Contacted	
Method Of Contact	
Reason	

Notes

Student Name	
Parents Name	
Address	
Phone Number	Home: Work:
Email	

Date	
Person Contacted	
Method Of Contact	
Reason	
Notes	

Date	
Person Contacted	
Method Of Contact	
Reason	
Notes	

Date	
Person Contacted	
Method Of Contact	
Reason	
Notes	

Date	
Person Contacted	
Method Of Contact	
Reason	
Notes	

Date	
Person Contacted	
Method Of Contact	
Reason	
Notes	

Student Name	
Parents Name	
Address	
Phone Number	Home: Work:
Email	

Date	
Person Contacted	
Method Of Contact	
Reason	
Notes	

Date	
Person Contacted	
Method Of Contact	
Reason	
Notes	

Date	
Person Contacted	
Method Of Contact	
Reason	
Notes	

Date	
Person Contacted	
Method Of Contact	
Reason	
Notes	

Date	
Person Contacted	
Method Of Contact	
Reason	
Notes	

Student Name	
Parents Name	
Address	
Phone Number	Home: Work:
Email	

Date	
Person Contacted	
Method Of Contact	
Reason	
Notes	

Date	
Person Contacted	
Method Of Contact	
Reason	
Notes	

Date	
Person Contacted	
Method Of Contact	
Reason	
Notes	

Date	
Person Contacted	
Method Of Contact	
Reason	
Notes	

Date	
Person Contacted	
Method Of Contact	
Reason	
Notes	

Student Name	
Parents Name	
Address	
Phone Number	Home: Work:
Email	

Date	
Person Contacted	
Method Of Contact	
Reason	
Notes	

Date	
Person Contacted	
Method Of Contact	
Reason	
Notes	

Date	
Person Contacted	
Method Of Contact	
Reason	
Notes	

Date	
Person Contacted	
Method Of Contact	
Reason	
Notes	

Date	
Person Contacted	
Method Of Contact	
Reason	
Notes	

Student Name	
Parents Name	
Address	
Phone Number	Home: Work:
Email	

Date	
Person Contacted	
Method Of Contact	
Reason	
Notes	

Date	
Person Contacted	
Method Of Contact	
Reason	
Notes	

Date	
Person Contacted	
Method Of Contact	
Reason	
Notes	

Date	
Person Contacted	
Method Of Contact	
Reason	
Notes	

Date	
Person Contacted	
Method Of Contact	
Reason	
Notes	

Student Name	
Parents Name	
Address	
Phone Number	Home: Work:
Email	

Date	
Person Contacted	
Method Of Contact	
Reason	
Notes	

Date	
Person Contacted	
Method Of Contact	
Reason	
Notes	

Date	
Person Contacted	
Method Of Contact	
Reason	

Notes

Date	
Person Contacted	
Method Of Contact	
Reason	

Notes

Date	
Person Contacted	
Method Of Contact	
Reason	

Notes

Student Name	
Parents Name	
Address	
Phone Number	Home: Work:
Email	

Date	
Person Contacted	
Method Of Contact	
Reason	
Notes	

Date	
Person Contacted	
Method Of Contact	
Reason	
Notes	

Date	
Person Contacted	
Method Of Contact	
Reason	

Notes

Date	
Person Contacted	
Method Of Contact	
Reason	

Notes

Date	
Person Contacted	
Method Of Contact	
Reason	

Notes

Student Name	
Parents Name	
Address	
Phone Number	Home: Work:
Email	

Date	
Person Contacted	
Method Of Contact	
Reason	
Notes	

Date	
Person Contacted	
Method Of Contact	
Reason	
Notes	

Date	
Person Contacted	
Method Of Contact	
Reason	
Notes	

Date	
Person Contacted	
Method Of Contact	
Reason	
Notes	

Date	
Person Contacted	
Method Of Contact	
Reason	
Notes	

Student Name	
Parents Name	
Address	
Phone Number	Home: Work:
Email	

Date	
Person Contacted	
Method Of Contact	
Reason	
Notes	

Date	
Person Contacted	
Method Of Contact	
Reason	
Notes	

Date	
Person Contacted	
Method Of Contact	
Reason	
Notes	

Date	
Person Contacted	
Method Of Contact	
Reason	
Notes	

Date	
Person Contacted	
Method Of Contact	
Reason	
Notes	

Student Name	
Parents Name	
Address	
Phone Number	Home: Work:
Email	

Date	
Person Contacted	
Method Of Contact	
Reason	
Notes	

Date	
Person Contacted	
Method Of Contact	
Reason	
Notes	

Date	
Person Contacted	
Method Of Contact	
Reason	
Notes	

Date	
Person Contacted	
Method Of Contact	
Reason	
Notes	

Date	
Person Contacted	
Method Of Contact	
Reason	
Notes	

Student Name	
Parents Name	
Address	
Phone Number	Home: Work:
Email	

Date	
Person Contacted	
Method Of Contact	
Reason	
Notes	

Date	
Person Contacted	
Method Of Contact	
Reason	
Notes	

Date	
Person Contacted	
Method Of Contact	
Reason	
Notes	

Date	
Person Contacted	
Method Of Contact	
Reason	
Notes	

Date	
Person Contacted	
Method Of Contact	
Reason	
Notes	

Student Name	
Parents Name	
Address	
Phone Number	Home: Work:
Email	

Date	
Person Contacted	
Method Of Contact	
Reason	
Notes	

Date	
Person Contacted	
Method Of Contact	
Reason	
Notes	

Date	
Person Contacted	
Method Of Contact	
Reason	
Notes	

Date	
Person Contacted	
Method Of Contact	
Reason	
Notes	

Date	
Person Contacted	
Method Of Contact	
Reason	
Notes	

Student Name	
Parents Name	
Address	
Phone Number	Home: Work:
Email	

Date	
Person Contacted	
Method Of Contact	
Reason	
Notes	

Date	
Person Contacted	
Method Of Contact	
Reason	
Notes	

Date	
Person Contacted	
Method Of Contact	
Reason	
Notes	

Date	
Person Contacted	
Method Of Contact	
Reason	
Notes	

Date	
Person Contacted	
Method Of Contact	
Reason	
Notes	

Made in the USA
Las Vegas, NV
26 August 2021